WHAT·DO·WE·KNOW ABOUT HINDUISM·?

ANITA GANERI

PETER BEDRICK BOOKS

NEW YORK

Published by
PETER BEDRICK BOOKS
156 Fifth Avenue,
New York, NY 10010

© Macdonald Young Books Ltd 1995

Library of Congress
Cataloging-in-Publication Data

Ganeri, Anita, 1961 –

    What do we know about Hinduism? / Anita Ganeri.
        p.   cm.
    Includes index.
    ISBN 0-87226-385-1
    1. Hinduism.   I. Title.
BL1202.G38   1996   95-51827
294.5--dc20   CIP

Designer and illustrator: Celia Hart
Commissioning editor: Debbie Fox
Copy editor: Caroline Arthur
Picture research: Valerie Mulcahy
Series design: David West
                Children's Book Design

Photograph acknowledgements: Front and back cover: Dinodia/Trip; Ancient
Art & Architecture Collection, p17(tl); The Bridgeman Art Library, London,
endpapers (British Library, London), pp38 (Freud Museum, London), 39(t)
(Victoria & Albert Museum, London); CIRCA Photo Library, pp9, 15(t), 17(b),
27(l); Dinodia/Trip, pp21(t), 32(r), 35(c), 43; Robert Harding Picture Library,
pp12(l), 20(l) (Tony Gervis), 32(l) (J H C Wilson), 35(t), 35(b) (J H C Wilson),
41(b); Michael Holford, pp13(b), 14, 16; The Hutchison Library, pp31(b),
33(r) (MacIntyre), 37; Magnum, pp15(b) (Raghu Rai), 26 (Abbas);
Bipinchandra J Mistry, p28(r); Chris Oxlade, p36(l); Ann & Bury Peerless,
pp13(t), 12(r), 18, 19(t) (br), 21(b), 22, 25(t), 27(r), 28(l), 29(t) (b), 31(c), 34,
36(r), 39(b), 42; Rex Features/ Sipa-Press, p31(t); Peter Sanders, pp23(t), 24,
25(b); Spectrum Colour Library, p40; Tony Stone Images, pp8(l) (Anthony
Cassidy), 8(r), 41(t) (David Hanson); Trip, pp20(r) (Helene Rogers), 23(b)
(Helene Rogers), 30 (W Jacobs), 33(l) (Helene Rogers).

Printed in Hong Kong by Wing King Tong
First edition, 1996
Second printing, 1998

Endpapers: This painting shows a scene
from the *Ramayana*, in which Rama and
Sita are living in exile in the forest.

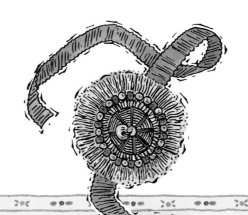

· CONTENTS ·

WHO·ARE·THE·HINDUS?

Hindus are followers of a religion known as Hinduism. It was given this name by Western scholars in the 19th century, but Hindus themselves call their code of beliefs *sanatana dharma,* which means 'eternal law' or 'eternal teaching'. The name 'Hindu' was first used by the ancient Persians over 2,000 years ago to describe the people living to the east of the River Indus (now Pakistan). Hinduism is one of the oldest and largest religions in the world. It began thousands of years ago in India, where most of its followers still live. It is a very flexible, practical religion, allowing people to worship in many different ways, depending on their own particular needs.

HOLY MAN
This man is a *sadhu*, or Hindu holy man. Sadhus give up all their own possessions to live a life of prayer and meditation. They wander from place to place, receiving gifts of food and money from local people and giving blessings in return. Sadhus are often seen in Indian towns and villages.

HINDUISM IN BALI
Bali is a tiny island in Indonesia. Most of Indonesia is Muslim, but Hinduism has flourished in Bali for over 1,200 years. Each village has several Hindu temples, such as the one above, where religious and official events take place.

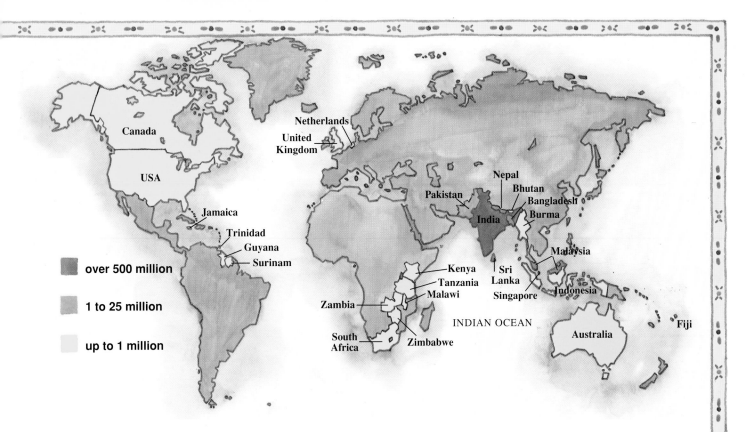

over 500 million

1 to 25 million

up to 1 million

Canada

USA

Jamaica

Trinidad
Guyana
Surinam

Netherlands
United Kingdom

Pakistan
Nepal
Bhutan
Bangladesh
India
Burma

Kenya
Tanzania
Malawi

Sri Lanka

Malaysia

Singapore
Indonesia

Zambia

South Africa
Zimbabwe

INDIAN OCEAN

Australia

Fiji

THE HINDU WORLD

Two thirds of Hindus live in India and in the neighboring countries of Pakistan, Nepal, Bhutan, Sri Lanka, Bangladesh and Burma, but there are Hindu communities all over the world. About 1,000 years ago, traders took Hinduism to Malaysia, Thailand and other parts of South-East Asia, where many Hindus still live and work today. More recently, Hindus have gone to live in Britain, Canada and the USA. The Hindus living in Africa and the West Indies are descendants of Indian laborers who settled in these countries in the 19th century.

 ## NUMBERS OF HINDUS

There are about 700 million Hindus in the world. The vast majority live in India, where eight people in ten are Hindus.

It is said that you are born a Hindu; you cannot become one. But non-Hindus are free to follow the teachings of Hinduism and use them as guides for living their lives.

HINDU WORSHIPERS

Wherever Hindus have settled, they have taken their beliefs with them. These Hindus are worshiping in a temple in Britain, where thousands of Hindus now live. Many came to Britain in the 1950's from countries that were previously part of the British Empire. Most young Hindus in Britain have been born and brought up there, but Hindu traditions and culture are very important to them. The temple is a good place to learn about their faith.

T I M E L I N E

THE DEVELOPMENT OF HINDUISM

c. 2500BC	*c.* 1500BC	*c.* 1500–1000BC	*c.* 800BC	*c.* 500BC	400BC–AD400
The Indus Valley Civilization is at the height of its power. Its two centers are the cities of Harappa and Mohenjo Daro.	The Aryan people begin to invade India from the north-west. Their Vedic religion mixes with Indus Valley beliefs to form the basis of Hinduism.	The *Rig Veda* and the other three Vedas are used by the Aryan priests in their rituals. The caste system develops.	The *Upanishads* are composed, although they are not written down for several hundred more years.	The Buddha spreads his teachings all over India, laying the foundations of Buddhism. The Jain religion is founded by Mahavira.	Large parts of the two epic poems, the *Mahabharata* and the *Ramayana,* are composed.

Indus Valley Civilization seal

Buddha

AD1828	AD1784	1600s–1700s AD	AD1632	1570s AD	AD1556–1605
Ram Mohan Roy founds the Brahmo Samaj (Society of God), which seeks to reform Hinduism.	Under the India Act, the British gain political control of India and it becomes part of the British Empire. This marks the start of the British Raj (rule).	The British, French, Dutch and Portuguese bring Christianity to India.	The Mughal emperor Shah Jehan begins building the Taj Mahal in Agra, as a memorial to his dead wife, Mumtaz.	The poet Tulsi Das writes his great work, the *Ram Charit Manas,* based on the *Ramayana.*	Reign of the Mughal emperor Akbar the Great. He forms his own new religion, which mixes Muslim, Hindu and Christian beliefs.

AD1857					
The first Indian War of Independence against the British.					

The Taj Mahal

The flag of India

AD1869	AD1875	AD1876	AD1897	AD1910	AD1947
Birth of Mahatma Gandhi, one of the leaders of India's struggle for freedom from the British.	The Arya Samaj, another Hindu movement, is formed.	Queen Victoria is proclaimed Empress of India. She never visits India.	Swami Vivekananda establishes the Ramakrishna Mission in India. Its headquarters are in Calcutta.	Sri Aurobindo, a holy man and former revolutionary, starts a religious center in Pondicherry, India.	India gains independence from the British but is partitioned into Hindu India and Muslim Pakistan.

AD320–550	c. AD700–800	c. AD800	c. AD900
India is ruled by the Gupta kings and enjoys the 'golden age' of Hinduism.	The Hindu Mataram kingdom is established in Java, Indonesia.	The great Hindu philosopher Shankaracharya writes and teaches about the *Upanishads*.	The Chola kings rule over South India. Many beautiful temples are built.

Gupta coin

			AD1001
			The Muslims begin to invade India from the north-west and to spread their religion of Islam.

AD1526	AD1469	AD1336–1555	c. AD1050
The Muslim Mughal Empire is founded in India.	The birth of Guru Nanak, founder of the Sikh religion.	The Hindu kingdom of Vijayanagar thrives in South India, despite the arrival of the Muslims in the north.	Ramanuja, the Hindu philosopher, teaches in South India.

Mahatma Gandhi

AD1948	1950s–1960s AD	1990s AD
Mahatma Gandhi is assassinated on his way to a prayer meeting. His final words are '*He Ram*' ('Oh God').	Many Hindus leave India to live in Britain, Canada and the USA.	Fighting breaks out between Muslims and Hindus in Ayodhya, the birthplace of Rama. The Bharatiya Janata Party, a Hindu political party, grows in power.

PARTITION OF INDIA

India gained independence from British rule on 15 August 1947. But there was a high price to pay for its freedom. The Muslim League, which spoke up for the rights of Muslims living in India, had campaigned for a separate country for India's Muslims. So India was divided into mainly Hindu India and mainly Muslim Pakistan. The newly created country of Pakistan was itself divided, for most of the Muslims lived in the western state of Punjab (West Pakistan) and in the eastern state of Bengal (East Pakistan), on opposite sides of India. The partition of India caused terrible suffering. Millions of people were killed in violence between Hindus and Muslims and millions were left homeless. In 1971, East Pakistan became the independent, mainly Muslim country of Bangladesh.

Swastika

SIGN OF PEACE

The swastika is an ancient Hindu symbol of peace. It is often drawn on cards and invitations and woven into textiles to bring good luck. In the 20th century, the German Nazis took the swastika symbol, reversed it and turned it into a symbol of evil. To Hindus, however, it has exactly the opposite meaning.

H O W · D I D HINDUISM · B E G I N ? ·

Although we know that Hinduism is one of the world's oldest religions, there is no fixed date for when it began. Its roots go back over 4,000 years to the time of the great Indus Valley Civilization, which thrived along the River Indus in the west of India. Many clay figures have been found among the ruins of the Indus Valley cities. Some show gods and goddesses that are similar to those worshiped by Hindus today. The Indus Valley Civilization collapsed in about 2000BC. Around 500 years later, a group of people called the Aryans began to arrive in India from the north-west. Their religion combined with the Indus Valley religion to form the basis of Hinduism. The Aryans worshiped many gods, mostly linked with nature and the world around them. The religious hymns recited by their priests are still some of the most sacred Hindu texts.

INDUS VALLEY CIVILIZATION
The two great cities of the Indus Valley Civilization were Harappa and Mohenjo Daro. Archaeologists began excavating the cities in the 1920's. Each had a hilltop fort, or citadel (see below), used as a temple and government building. Among the artifacts found were hundreds of stone seals like the one on the right, used by merchants to mark their goods. Many show religious scenes or sacred animals such as bulls and elephants.

Seal showing a bull

KING OR PRIEST?
The carved stone head above was found among the ruins of Mohenjo Daro. It may be the head of a king, or it may be a priest, with his eyes closed in meditation. Masks and headdresses which may have belonged to the priests of the Indus Valley have also been found.

The Aryans performed elaborate rituals to keep the gods happy, so that they would grant favors such as good health or a good harvest. At the center of the most important rituals was the sacrificial fire. The priest threw offerings of grains, spices, butter and milk into the fire. Goats and horses were also sacrificed to the gods. The Aryans believed that the fire acted as a bridge between this world and heaven, carrying their sacrifices up to the gods. As they performed the sacrifices, the priests sang and chanted hymns and spells. They had to be word perfect. Any mistakes meant that the sacrifice would not work and the whole ritual would have to begin all over again, which could take several days.

AGNI
The sculpture above shows Agni, the god of fire and sacrifice, one of the most important Aryan gods. Agni was also worshiped as the god of the home because he was found in the fireplace of every household.

INDRA
In the picture below, the god Indra is riding across the sky on his white battle elephant. Indra was the Aryan god of war, famous for his bravery and strength. He was also the god of storms and thunder. His special weapon was the *vajra*, or thunderbolt, which he used to destroy his enemies. Indra was the most popular Aryan god; many hymns were sung in his praise.

There are many different ways of being a Hindu. Some Hindus worship every day. Others do not take part in any formal worship. There are no set rules. But most Hindus share the same basic beliefs. One important belief is reincarnation, which means that your soul is reborn in another body, human or animal, when you die. You can be reborn many times, in a cycle of death and rebirth called *samsara*. The aim of a Hindu's life is to break free of this cycle and to reach *moksha*, or salvation. By leading a good life, you can be reborn into a higher form and move closer to *moksha*. But this depends on your actions and their results, which are known as *karma*.

SEEKING SALVATION

These Hindus are bathing in the sacred River Ganges. They believe that its water is holy and that by bathing in it and drinking from it they will wash away their sins and come closer to *moksha*. Bathing plays an important part in Hinduism. Many temples have tanks, wells or taps where worshipers can bathe so that they are clean and pure when they enter.

Sacred symbol, 'Om'

SACRED SOUND

This is the sound 'Om', written in Hindi script. Hindus believe it is a symbol of spiritual perfection. It is recited at the beginning of prayers, blessings and readings from the sacred books, and also used during meditation (see page 27).

MONASTERY SCHOOLS

These boys are being educated at an *ashram*, a cross between a school, a university and a monastery. Here they learn about their faith from priests and religious teachers called *gurus*. Ashrams also provide shelter and a place to study and meditate for wandering holy men. Devout Hindus who want peace, quiet and time away from the hustle and bustle of the world go there for spiritual guidance. The bond between a guru and his pupils is very strong. The pupils always treat their guru with great respect.

A WAY OF LIVING

Hinduism is not a fixed, formal religion, set apart from ordinary life. It affects everything a Hindu does, from working in the fields or office to cooking *chapattis* for a meal. Hinduism is very much part of everyday life. Most Hindu taxi or rickshaw drivers have a picture of a god or holy man in their cabs. The gods and goddesses even appear in Hindi films. Hindus try to live their lives according to a code of behavior called *dharma*. This means doing their duty to their family and friends, working hard and telling the truth.

 ## PATHS TO FOLLOW

There are four paths or ways Hindus can follow to reach *moksha*. They can choose whichever path is best suited to them.

The Path of Devotion – prayer, worship and devotion to a personal god

The Path of Knowledge – study and learning, with a guru's guidance

The Path of Right Action – acting selflessly, without any thought of reward for yourself

The Path of Yoga – yoga (see page 27) and meditation.

WHICH·ARE ·THE·MAIN· GODS·AND GODDESSES?

Most Hindus believe in a supreme soul or spirit, called Brahman. Brahman does not have any shape or form, but is all around, all the time, in everything. The gods and goddesses of Hinduism represent different aspects, or characteristics, of Brahman. The three main gods are Brahma, the creator, Vishnu, the protector, and Shiva, the destroyer. Vishnu and Shiva are very popular gods, worshiped by millions of Hindus, with temples dedicated to them all over India. There is only one temple dedicated to Brahma. A Hindu may worship one god, many gods or none at all. Many people find it easier to have a picture of a god in their mind as they worship. Families often have their own special gods which they have worshiped for many generations as a family tradition.

BRAHMA

Hindu gods and goddesses are often painted or carved with several heads or arms to show their special qualities. This statue of Brahma has four faces, although you can only see three at a time. The four faces show that Brahma rules over the four points of the compass. Brahma is also shown with four arms, in which he holds the sacred books and the rosary and water flask of a holy man. Brahma is the creator of the universe and the god of wisdom. His wife is Saraswati, the goddess of art, music and literature. She is usually shown holding a book and a *vina*, a type of musical instrument, in her hands.

SHIVA

In paintings and statues Shiva, the destroyer of the world, is often dancing. The dance is a way of showing the energy flowing through the world, which causes day and night, the seasons and birth and death. As Shiva dances, he treads the dwarf of ignorance underfoot.

Dancing Shiva

VISHNU

Vishnu is the protector of the universe. He rides on the huge eagle, Garuda, with his wife, Lakshmi, the goddess of beauty and good fortune. Vishnu is often shown with four arms, in which he holds a conch shell, a lotus flower, a discus and a club.

AVATARS

Vishnu has come to earth ten times, in ten different forms, or *avatars*, to save the world:

Matsya, the fish

Kurma, the tortoise

Varaha, the boar

Narasimha, the man–lion

Vamana, the dwarf

Parashurama, the warrior

Lord Rama

Lord Krishna

Buddha

Kalki, the rider on the white horse, who is yet to come.

MOUNTS OF THE GODS

The gods and goddesses all have their own special animals to ride. Brahma rides on a goose and Saraswati on a peacock or swan. Vishnu rides on an eagle or on a gigantic snake. Shiva rides on the great bull, Nandi, shown below. Every Shiva temple has its own statue of Nandi standing guard over it.

Apart from the three main Hindu gods, there are thousands of other gods and goddesses. Some are worshiped all over India. Others are popular only in particular regions or even in particular villages. The most important of these deities are Rama and Krishna, two of Vishnu's *avatars*, and the goddess Parvati, the wife of Shiva. Rama and Krishna are very popular, much-loved gods. Many people worship them because they feel they are easier to approach than some of the higher gods. The goddess Parvati is worshiped in many different forms: as the gentle Mother Goddess, as the bloodthirsty goddess Kali, and as Durga, the goddess of war. Like many Hindu deities, Parvati is a mixture of good and evil, kindness and cruelty, life and death.

RAMA AND SITA

The scene on the left shows Rama and his wife, Sita, in the forest with their faithful servant, the monkey god Hanuman. Rama is the hero of the great epic poem, the *Ramayana* (see page 29), which tells of his victory over the evil demon king, Ravana. Rama is worshiped as an ideal human being – brave, handsome, loyal and kind. He is a great hero, a good husband and a just king. The monkey god, Hanuman, who helps Rama defeat Ravana, is worshiped as a god in his own right.

SUN AND MOON

Surya, the sun god, rides his golden chariot across the sky each morning, bringing light and warmth to the world after the dark night. His wife is Ushas, the goddess of dawn.

Surya, the sun god

Chandra, the moon god

As night falls, it is the turn of Chandra, the moon god, to drive his silver chariot across the sky as the gleaming moon.

KRISHNA

Krishna, the eighth *avatar* of Vishnu, is one of the most popular Hindu gods. He is famous for his mischievous nature and for the tricks he plays on his friends. He also performs miracles, such as lifting up a huge mountain to shelter his companions during a torrential downpour of rain. He is the hero of many adventures. Krishna is usually shown with dark blue or black skin and carrying or playing a flute. He is often surrounded by cows and by *gopis* (milkmaids).

DURGA

Durga is the warlike form of the goddess Parvati. Here she is riding on the back of a fierce tiger, with a different weapon in each of her ten hands. She is about to plunge her sword into a buffalo, really a terrible demon in disguise, to fulfill a task set her by the other gods.

Ganesha

GANESHA

Ganesha, the elephant-headed god, removes obstacles and is the patron god of travellers. Hindus pray to Ganesha before beginning anything new, such as starting a new job or moving to a new house. Ganesha is the son of Shiva and Parvati. He rides on a mouse or rat.

· HOW · DO · HINDU · FAMILIES · LIVE ? ·

Family life is very important to Hindus. Traditionally, Hindus live as part of a large family, with parents, grandparents, children, aunts and uncles all together under the same roof. This is called an extended family. The house can get very noisy and crowded, but no one ever feels lonely. Everyone shares in the family duties and chores and looks after one another. Children learn about their religion from their parents and grandparents and are also taught to respect their elders. They greet their grandparents, aunts and uncles by bowing and touching their feet as a sign of respect. In return, they receive a blessing.

JOINT FAMILY

This Hindu girl has just got married and is seen here with her new husband and members of her family. After her wedding, she will leave her own family and go to live in her husband's family home with his parents and brothers and their wives. Every member of a Hindu family has a special title to show their position in the family. Hindus very rarely call people by their first names. For example, you would call your father's younger brother *chachaji* and his wife *chachiji*, your father's younger sister *buaji* and her husband *phuphaji*. It can get very complicated.

CASTE SYSTEM

Hindus are divided into four classes, or castes, traditionally based on the jobs they do. The highest caste is that of the Brahmins, or priests. Next come Kshatriyas – the warriors and nobles. Below them are Vaishyas, or merchants, then Shudras, or ordinary laborers, such as these potters. A fifth group of people were considered to be outside the caste system because they did the dirtiest jobs. You are born into a particular caste, but after you die you can be reborn into a higher or lower caste, depending on your *karma*.

Sweets

VEGETARIAN FOOD

Hindus have respect for all living things. Many are vegetarians, because they do not believe in killing animals to eat. A typical meal consists of several spicy vegetable dishes, with *dahi* (yogurt) and flat bread or rice, eaten from banana leaves or large metal trays. People eat with their fingers, using their right hands only, because their left hands are considered unclean. To drink there is water, sweet tea or a yogurt drink called *lassi*.

INDIAN SWEETS

Many Hindus have a very sweet tooth and sweets are given as gifts at weddings and other festival times. The sweets are made from milk, cheese, nuts, coconut and sugar. Two of the favorite sweets are almond-flavored *badam burfi* and syrupy *rasgulla*. People make sweets at home or buy them from sweet-shops.

SACRED COWS

Wherever you go in India, you can see cows wandering through the streets, munching on vegetable scraps and getting in the way of the traffic. Hindus believe that cows are sacred animals because they produce milk, a very precious source of food. No Hindu will harm or kill a cow, nor eat beef.

NAMING NAMES

Many Hindu children are named after gods and goddesses, or have names with other special meanings related to their religion.

Boys
Rajendra – Lord Indra
Janardhan – another name for Krishna
Anand – joy, bliss
Mahesh – Lord, God

Girls
Devi – goddess
Puja – prayer, worship
Vandana – worshiper
Lakshmi – Vishnu's wife

WHERE · DO · HINDUS · WORSHIP?

Hindus worship in buildings called *mandir*, or temples. There are temples all over India and many temples have also been set up in other places where Hindus have settled. Temples are usually dedicated to a particular god, goddess or holy man. They are seen as the earthly home of the deity, whose presence is shown by an image or statue in a shrine in the innermost, holiest part of the temple building. Many Hindus also worship at home, in a room or part of a room which has been turned into a shrine. But there are no set rules about where Hindus should worship. Some people visit the temple every day; others only visit at special times, such as festivals.

TEMPLES

This is the entrance gateway of a temple in Kanchipuram, South India, dedicated to Shiva. The gateway is called a *gopuram* and is decorated all over with carvings of gods and goddesses. In North India, temples are laid out in a different way. The tallest part of the temple is a pointed tower called a *shikhara*, built over the inner sanctum of the temple.

Temple bell

TEMPLE BELL

Hindu temples are noisy, lively places, filled with the sound of people praying, singing and chanting from the sacred books. Worshipers ring the temple bell as they enter the temple and again as they leave.

STREET SHRINES

As well as grand temples, there are also small shrines on many street corners, where Hindus can worship on their way to work or school. They might say a short prayer or offer some flowers or sweets to the god. This street shrine is dedicated to Shiva, who is represented by a stone carving called a *lingam* (see page 38). The bull, Nandi, stands guard. Shrines are also a common sight in farmers' fields and in villages.

MORE TEMPLES

The only temple in India dedicated to Brahma is in the town of Pushkar in Rajasthan, western India. At the entrance is a goose, Brahma's special animal, which is said to have chosen the site of the temple.

A group of beautiful stone temples stands along the seashore at Mahabalipuram in South India. They were carved in the seventh century AD. The town is still famous for the skill of its sculptors and stonemasons.

Temples at Mahabalipuram

WORSHIP AT HOME

Many Hindus set aside a special place in their home as a shrine where the family can go to worship. This may be a room, a corner of a room or simply a shelf, with a statue or picture of the family's favorite god or goddess. This shrine is dedicated to Saraswati, the goddess of art and music, who is the wife of Brahma. The brass pots on the floor contain offerings of leaves, flowers and sweets which will be presented to the goddess for her blessing.

· HOW · DO · HINDUS · WORSHIP ?

When Hindus visit a temple or shrine, it is not just to pray but also to have a *darshana* of the god or goddess. This means a sight of the image or statue that shows the presence of the god or goddess in the inner sanctum. The worshipers then perform a ceremony called *puja*. They offer flowers, fruit, sweets and holy Ganges water to the deity, in return for his or her blessing. There is no set service or fixed time for worship in a temple. Hindus can visit whenever they like, alone or with friends or relations. Sometimes a whole village arranges an outing to a temple in a nearby town.

THE INNER SANCTUM

A priest sits near the image of the god or goddess in the inner sanctum of the temple. He is the only person allowed so close to the image. He takes the worshipers' offerings and does the *puja* for them. Then he marks their foreheads with a red sign of blessing, called a *tilaka*.

TEMPLE OFFERINGS

This stall is selling offerings of flowers, bananas, incense and colored powders for worshipers to buy before they go into the temple. There are stalls like this outside most Indian temples. These offerings are known as *prasad*. The priest takes them from the worshipers and offers them to the god to be blessed. Then he gives them back to the worshipers, to carry the god's blessing to them. A tray of small lighted lamps, called *arati*, may also be circled in front of the god for his blessing.

IN THE TEMPLE

Before Hindus can enter a temple they must take their shoes off and women must cover their heads as a mark of respect. These worshipers are waiting with their offerings for a *darshana* of the god Hanuman. You can see their trays of flower garlands and lamps. As part of their worship, people walk slowly around the shrine, always in a clockwise direction. This is so that they keep their right hands facing towards the inner sanctum and the god.

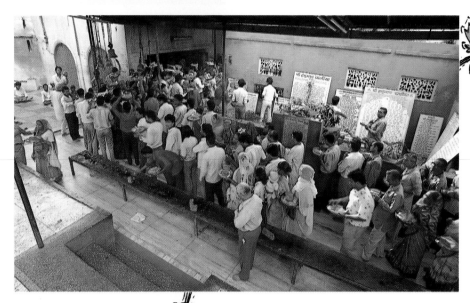

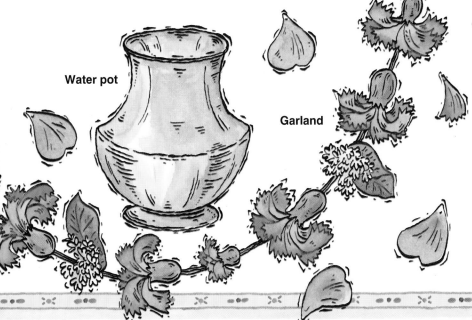

Water pot

Garland

BLESSING

Many prayers and passages from the sacred books are chanted or sung during worship. This short prayer is called the Gayatri Mantra. It is chanted in the morning, as the sun rises.

'We meditate upon the brilliance and glory of the god of the sun which lights up the heavens and the earth. May he inspire us and bless us.'

·WHO·ARE· ·HINDU· HOLY·MEN·?

Hindu holy men include religious teachers, priests and people who have given up their homes and possessions to lead a life of prayer and meditation. Some holy men live as wandering monks. They are called *sannyasins*. Others go to an *ashram* (monastery school) to study with a *guru*, or teacher, and learn how to become teachers themselves. A person who is very learned in religion is called a *pandit*. Some Hindus worship holy men, instead of a god or goddess, and there are many temples dedicated to them, just as there are to the gods.

HOLY MAN

You can tell by the horizontal marks on his forehead that this *sadhu*, or holy man, is a follower of Shiva. Followers of Vishnu have vertical marks on their foreheads. The sadhu is wearing a rosary of sacred beads and a saffron-colored cloth. Saffron is a holy color. He has let his hair and beard grow very long. The sadhu is meditating on the banks of the River Ganges. He has very few belongings of his own, but is given food and money by other worshipers.

HOLY WORDS

Here are some words spoken by famous Hindu holy men:

'The various religions that exist in the world, although they differ in the form of worship they take, are really all one.'
Swami Vivekananda

'I have nothing new to teach the world. Truth and non-violence are as old as the hills.'
Mahatma Gandhi

'A person who accepts a gift from the gods and does not repay it is a thief.'

Sri Aurobindo

RAMAKRISHNA MISSION

The temple below is part of the Ramakrishna Mission in India. It was founded in 1897 by Swami Vivekananda, a follower of a holy man called Ramakrishna. He taught that all religions were equal and believed not only in the Hindu gods but in Jesus Christ and Muhammad, the founder of Islam. The mission not only spreads Ramakrishna's message but also runs schools and hospitals all over India.

YOGA AND MEDITATION

Many Hindu holy men, and ordinary Hindus too, use yoga exercises and meditation to help train their bodies and minds towards *moksha*. The design below is called a *yantra*. People concentrate hard on yantras to help them focus their minds while they are meditating. They may also repeat a word or phrase over and over again.

BRAHMINS AND PRIESTS

Each temple has its own priest, who performs the *puja* ceremony and looks after the image of the god or goddess. The priest also helps people to read and study the holy books and to learn more about their religion. Most Hindu families have their own family priest. He comes to their home to conduct the ceremonies that take place at the time of a baby's birth, a wedding or a death. Priests come from the Brahmin caste.

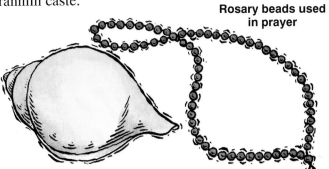

Rosary beads used in prayer

Sacred conch shell

Yantra

· WHICH · ARE · THE · HINDUS' · SACRED · BOOKS ?

The oldest Hindu sacred books date back to the time of the Aryans, more than 3,000 years ago. These are four collections of hymns, prayers and magic spells, called the *Vedas*. The oldest and most sacred is the *Rig Veda*, the 'Song of Knowledge'. It contains over 1,000 hymns. The other most important Hindu texts are the *Upanishads* and two long poems, the *Mahabharata* and the *Ramayana*. The *Vedas* and *Upanishads* are called *shruti*, or 'heard', texts. It is believed that a group of wise men heard them directly from Brahman, long ago. The other texts are known as *shmriti*, or 'remembered'. They were composed by people and passed on. For thousands of years, none of the sacred texts were written down. They were learned by heart and passed down by word of mouth.

THE UPANISHADS

The *Upanishads* were composed in about 800BC. They are made up of sacred teachings given by gurus to their pupils, using parables and stories to get a message across. While the *Vedas* are about worshiping the gods through fire and sacrifice, the *Upanishads* concentrate on the relationship between the individual person and Brahman. The picture on the right shows words from the *Upanishads* carved on the wall of a temple in Varanasi, India.

श्रीलक्ष्मीनारायण

एकही ईश्वर के अनेक नाम
स ब्रह्मा स शिवः सेन्द्रः सोऽक्षरः परमः स्वराट् ।
स एव विष्णुः स प्राणः स कालोऽग्निः स चन्द्रमाः॥ (केवल्य उप-१/७)
सर्वशक्तिमान् और समस्त जगत् का प्रकाशक वह परमात्मा ही ब्रह्मा (सृष्टि-कर्ता) है वही शिव रुद्र (विनाशकशक्ति) है, वही विष्णु (पालन करने वाली शक्ति) है वही इन्द्र है अविनाशी है वही सर्वव्यापक है, वही जगत् का जीवनाधार है वही काल है, अग्नि है, और चन्द्रमा है।
He is one and only one God
THAT ALMIGHTY, ALLPERVADING GOD IS BRAHMA, THE CREATIVE FORM, VISHNU THE PROTECTIVE FORM AND SHIVA, THE DESTRUCTIVE FORM. HE IS INDRA; HE IS IMMORTAL; HE IS SELF-EXISTENT AND SELF-EFFULGENT. HE IS LIFE-FORM, HE IS TIME, HE IS FIRE AND HE IS MOON. (K.UPANISHAD 1/8)

BHAGAVAD GITA

The *Bhagavad Gita* is the most important and most popular part of the *Mahabharata*, a very long poem with over 90,000 verses. The *Mahabharata* tells the story of a war between the Kauravas and the Pandavas, two closely related royal families, who both want to control the kingdom of Hastinapura, which rightfully belongs to the Pandavas. The *Bhagavad Gita*, the 'Song of the Lord', is set on the battlefield just before the fighting begins. It consists of a conversation between Arjuna, one of the Pandavas, and his charioteer, the god Krishna. You can see them on the left. Krishna is about to blow his conch shell to call the soldiers to battle. Arjuna tells Krishna how sad and frightened he feels about fighting his cousins, the Kauravas. Krishna replies that Arjuna must ignore his own feelings and simply do his duty as a warrior, because the way to *moksha* lies in unselfish action, not in thinking of oneself. Arjuna takes Krishna's advice and leads his soldiers into battle. The fighting lasts for 18 days, until the Kaurava army is completely destroyed.

SANSKRIT

The *Vedas* and *Upanishads* were spoken and later written down in Sanskrit. This was the ancient language of the Aryans and is the sacred language of India. The name 'Sanskrit' means 'perfected'. Sanskrit is believed to have special power for communicating with the gods. It is not spoken now except for religious purposes, but it is still studied by priests and scholars. Hindi, the modern language of India, developed from Sanskrit.

कर्मण्येवाधिकारस्ते
मा फलेषु कदाचन।
मा कर्मफलहेतुर्भूर्
मा ते संगोऽस्त्वकर्मणि ॥

You have a right to do your duty,
But you have no right to the fruits of your action.
Whatever the results of your actions,
Do not think of yourself as the cause.
And never choose the path of not doing your duty.

Bhagavad Gita (chapter 2 : verse 47)

THE RAMAYANA

The *Ramayana* tells the story of the god Rama and how he rescues his wife, Sita, from the evil demon, Ravana. You can read this story on pages 42–43. The poem was first composed over 2,000 years ago, but the most famous version of the tale was written in the 1570s by the poet Tulsi Das, who is shown here. The *Ramayana* was recently made into a serial for Indian television. People were so upset when it finished that a new ending was written to make it last longer.

· WHICH · ARE · THE · HINDUS' · SACRED · PLACES ?

Every year, millions of Hindus set off on special journeys, called pilgrimages, to holy places such as temples, mountains and rivers. They travel by plane, train, boat or ox cart. Some people walk, even though the journey might last for days or even weeks. There are many reasons for making a pilgrimage. A person might want to pray for something special, such as good health or the birth of a child, or to thank the gods for granting their wishes. Hindus also believe a visit to a sacred place will help them move closer to *moksha*. Many sacred places are connected to events in the lives of the gods, goddesses or holy men, or are famous for their beauty or healing qualities.

CROSSING PLACES

The map shows some of the most sacred places in India, including the seven holiest Hindu cities – Varanasi, Ayodhya, Mathura, Hardwar, Ujjain, Dwarka and Kanchipuram. These places are called *tirthas*, which means 'fords' or 'crossing places'. Hindus believe they are places where you can cross over from this world to *moksha*.

THE HOLY GANGES

Varanasi is the Hindus' holiest place of pilgrimage. Millions of people flock to the city to wash away their sins in the sacred River Ganges and to scatter the ashes of dead relations in the water. Hindus believe Varanasi is the best place to die. The pilgrims bathe from the crumbling stone steps, called *ghats*, along the riverbank. There are hundreds of temples in the city itself, mostly dedicated to Shiva. According to Hindu legend, Shiva chose Varanasi as his home on earth.

BATHING FAIRS

Every 12 years, in January or February, a huge fair is held at Allahabad. The exact date of the fair is fixed by an astrologer. Over two million pilgrims come to bathe at the place near the city where the River Ganges, the River Yamuna and the mythical River Saraswati flow together. So many pilgrims crowd into the town that a vast temporary camp is set up by the riverside to house everyone. This type of bathing fair is called a *kumbha mela*.

GANGES LEGEND

This is the story of how the River Ganges fell to earth. There was once a king called Bhagiratha, who begged Shiva to let the Ganges fall to earth so that its magical powers could bring his dead ancestors back to life. Shiva agreed to his request, but saw that the earth would shatter under the water's great weight. So he caught the Ganges in his hair, to break its fall, and let it trickle gently down to the Himalayas.

RAMESHWARAM

The picture above shows the magnificent hall of the famous Ramanathaswamy temple on the island of Rameshwaram, South India. Rama is said to have worshiped here after his battle with Ravana (see pages 42–43). Nowadays it is an important pilgrimage center for Hindus. This temple was begun in the 12th century AD.

MOUNTAIN HOMES

The mighty Himalayan mountains stretch across the north of India. They are the highest mountains in the world. Many of the mountains are holy places. For example, Mount Kailash is sacred to Shiva and Parvati. These pilgrims are making the difficult journey up to Gangotri, the source of the River Ganges, high up in the snow-capped mountains. To the west of Gangotri lies Yamunotri, the source of another sacred river, the Yamuna. The river flows out from a frozen lake.

WHAT·ARE THE·MAIN ·HINDU· FESTIVALS?

Hindu festivals are lively, joyful times when the whole family, community or village joins in the celebrations. There are hundreds of festivals throughout the year, large and small. Some celebrate the birthdays of god, or other important times in their lives. Other festivals are linked to the changing of the seasons, harvest time or events in the family. There are far too many festivals to celebrate them all, but most Hindus celebrate the main festivals of Diwali, Holi and Dussehra. A special *puja* is held at home or in the temple, sweets and gifts are exchanged, and there is often music and dancing. Festivals are also celebrated by Hindus living outside India. They are a good way for children to learn more about Hinduism and a time for friends and relations to get together.

LOCAL FESTIVALS
Many villages have their own festivals, to celebrate the rice or wheat harvest or to honor the village gods. These women are preparing offerings for a festival. Some local festivals are not religious. The annual kite-flying festival in western India, for example, is just for fun.

Kite

DIWALI
Diwali is one of the most important and joyful Hindu festivals. It is celebrated at the end of October or the beginning of November. Diwali is the Hindu festival of lights. People light rows of small oil lamps and place them by their doors and windows to guide Rama back home after his long exile (see page 42). Diwali is also a time for worshiping Lakshmi, the goddess of good fortune, and for businesses to start their new year's accounts. The Diwali celebrations last five days. People exchange cards and gifts of silver and new clothes. There are also fireworks to watch and plenty of special Diwali food to eat.

DUSSEHRA

The Dussehra festival is held in September. In eastern India, it celebrates Durga's victory over the buffalo demon. In other places, it marks Rama's victory over the demon king Ravana. This story is acted out as a play called the *Rama Lila*. On the last night of the play, the actor playing Rama fires a burning arrow into a gigantic paper-mâché figure of Ravana, like the ones in the photograph on the right. The figure is stuffed with firecrackers and explodes with a loud bang.

HOLI

Holi celebrates the coming of spring in March or April. It is the liveliest and messiest festival of the year. On Holi Eve, a bonfire is lit and a model of the wicked witch Holika is burned on it. On the next day, the fun begins. People wear their oldest clothes and throw colored water and powders all over each other. In the evening, they have a bath, change their clothes and then visit their relations to wish them a happy Holi.

Rakhi bracelets

RAKSHA BANDHAN

Raksha Bandhan is a family festival, which takes place in August. Sisters tie brightly colored bracelets, called *rakhis*, around their brothers' right wrists to show their affection. They also ask for their brothers' protection in the coming year. In return, brothers must give their sisters some money or a gift.

 HINDU CALENDAR

Hindu month	
Chaitra	March–April
Vaishakha	April–May
Jyaishtha	May–June
Ashadha	June–July
Shravana	July–August
Bhadra	August–September
Ashvina	September–October
Karttika	October–November
Margashirsha	November–December
Pausha	December–January
Magha	January–February
Phalguna	February–March

WHAT·ARE THE·MOST IMPORTANT ·TIMES·IN· A·HINDU'S ·LIFE?·

There are special ceremonies for many important times in a Hindu's life, such as being born, growing up, getting married and dying. These ceremonies are known as *samskaras*. Traditionally, there are 16 samskaras for a Hindu to celebrate, but very few people go through them all. The samskaras begin even before a baby is born, with prayers for the baby to be healthy and happy. Then there are ceremonies to mark the baby's birth, the first time it sees the sun and its first haircut. This is supposed to remove any bad *karma* from the baby's previous lives. The final samskaras take place when a person dies and is cremated.

HOROSCOPE

This is a Hindu horoscope drawn up for a newborn baby boy. It is written in Sanskrit. It shows the position of the stars and planets at the exact minute of the baby's birth. A priest draws up and reads the horoscope to tell the baby's future. This is done at the same time as the baby's naming ceremony, which usually takes place ten days after its birth. The priest may help to choose a name for the baby, based on its horoscope. Horoscopes are also used to fix favorable dates for weddings and other celebrations.

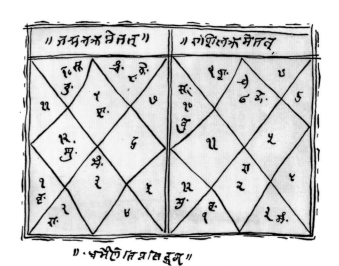

Baby boy's horoscope

SACRED THREAD

When a Hindu boy is nine or ten years old, he goes through his sacred thread ceremony. This is only for boys from the top three castes – Brahmins, Kshatriyas and Vaishyas. During the ceremony, the priest hangs a long loop of cotton thread over the boy's left shoulder and under his right arm. Prayers are said around the sacred fire. The ceremony is the boy's second 'birth' and the start of his adult life. He can now begin to study the sacred books and take on more responsibilities in his family. He is supposed to wear his sacred thread for the rest of his life.

A HINDU WEDDING

Many Hindus marry someone who has been chosen for them by their family. A Hindu wedding lasts for several days, with 15 different rituals to do. These include taking seven steps around the sacred fire, with a vow at each step. Here the bride and groom are exchanging flower garlands. The bride is dressed in a red silk wedding sari, embroidered with gold thread. She also wears beautiful jewelry and make-up. Instead of a wedding ring, the bride wears a special necklace.

 STAGES OF LIFE

A Hindu man's life is traditionally divided into four stages, called *ashramas*, with different duties at each stage. They are:

Brahmacharya	Life as a student
Grihastha	Married life
Vanaprastha	Retirement
Sannyasin	Life as a wandering holy man

DEATH AND CREMATION

When a Hindu dies, his or her body is taken to a cremation ground, where it is placed on a raised platform of logs and sandalwood. The person's eldest son or male relation lights the fire, while the priest chants from the holy books. As the body burns, the skull cracks and releases the person's soul for rebirth. Later, the ashes from the body are collected and, if possible, scattered in the River Ganges. Ten days of mourning follow the cremation. Every year, the anniversary of the person's death is marked with a ceremony.

· WHAT · IS · TRADITIONAL · HINDU · MEDICINE ?

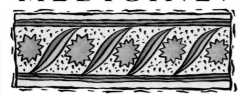

Traditional Hindu medicine is called Ayurveda, which means the 'science of long life'. Ayurveda has been practiced in India for thousands of years; the first textbooks were written in the first and fourth centuries AD. The Ayurvedic medicine practiced today has changed very little since that time. Ayurvedic doctors are called *vaidyas*. They believe that the human body is made up of three substances, called humors. These are bile, wind and mucous. Good health comes from getting the right balance of humors. If you get sick, it is because you have more of one type of humor than another, so any treatment aims to put the balance right. You can also achieve the right balance by eating healthy food, taking plenty of exercise and doing yoga. It is just as important to look after your mind as your body.

AYURVEDIC DISPENSARY

This dispensary, or pharmacy, in Pushkar, western India, is run by the government. It sells Ayurvedic medicines. Many Hindus prefer Ayurvedic remedies to modern drugs, but some people use a mixture of the two. The Ayurvedic chemist mixes up the ingredients recommended by the *vaidya* or suggests a remedy himself. Hundreds of different ingredients are used in Ayurvedic medicine. They include plants, herbs, spices and oils, each with its own special healing powers. Gemstones, metals and colors are also believed to have powers of healing.

SACRED PLANTS

This girl is tending a *tulsi* bush. Tulsi is a type of herb, like basil. It is a sacred plant, linked to Vishnu, and is believed to have great powers of healing. Many Hindus plant tulsi bushes in their houses to bring them good luck, and look after the plants with great care. Other sacred plants include *pipal* trees (fig trees) and *ashoka* trees. Ashoka leaves are often hung around the doorway of the family shrine.

Coriander

Cardamom

Here is a suggested Ayurvedic routine for living a healthier, happier life.

- Wake up early, before sunrise.
- Go to the toilet regularly.
- Have a bath every day.
- Eat breakfast before 8 a.m.
- Wash your hands before and after eating.
- Brush your teeth after meals.
- Take a short walk 15 minutes after a meal.
- Eat in silence and concentrate on your food.
- Eat slowly.
- Massage your gums every day with your finger.
- Drink plenty of water.
- Go to sleep before 10 p.m.

NATURAL MEDICINES

The herbs and spices shown above and on the right are all used in Ayurvedic medicine. Here are some of their healing properties:

Cardamom – good for the heart and lungs; relieves pain.

Cinnamon – gets rid of poisons in the body; good for the digestion.

Cloves – oil of cloves relieves toothache and colds.

Coriander – good for the digestion and for skin problems.

Garlic – good for rheumatism and ear problems.

Ginger – good for headaches, sore throats and colds.

Honey – good for the eyes and teeth; helps wounds heal.

Black pepper – good for loss of appetite and to reduce swelling.

STREET SELLER

This street seller has spread out his display of roots, dried plants and herbs on the pavement for passers-by to see. Many of these plants come from the mountains. The metal bar you can see in front of the street seller is his set of weighing scales.

Pepper

Ginger

· W H A T · I S · H I N D U · A R T · L I K E ?

Since ancient times, Hindu artists have created beautiful works of art, including giant sculptures, delicate carvings and exquisite paintings. Much of their art has been inspired by the Hindu religion. Most sculptures are of gods and goddesses, and many paintings and carvings tell stories from the sacred books. But Hindu art is not just for decoration. Many statues and sculptures are made specially for the holiest parts of a temple or a family shrine, where they show the presence of the gods on earth. Modern artists all over India still carve images of the gods in stone, wood and bronze. They use many of the same tools and techniques as the artists of long ago.

IMAGE OF A GOD

This statue of Vishnu is carved from ivory. Vishnu is sitting on the coils of the many-headed serpent, Sesha. Vishnu sleeps on Sesha while he waits for Brahma to create the world. In his four arms, he is holding the signs of his holiness and power. These are two sacred objects, a conch shell and a lotus flower, and two weapons, a club and a discus. He is wearing a tall, jeweled crown to show his status as a king.

SYMBOL OF SHIVA

In the inner sanctum of a temple dedicated to Shiva, you will not find a statue of the god but a simple stone or marble carving like the one below.
This is called a *lingam*. It is the symbol of Shiva's presence and power. Worshipers can buy much smaller *linga* (the plural of lingam) to take home or carry with them for luck.

Shiva lingam

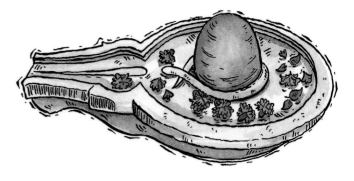

HINDU PAINTING

This painting shows Vishnu surrounded by his ten *avatars* (see page 17). From left to right they are (top row) Matsya the fish, Kurma the tortoise, Varaha the boar, (second row) Narasimha the man–lion, Vamana the dwarf, (third row) Parashurama the warrior, Rama, (bottom row) Krishna, the Buddha and Kalki, the horseman. The picture was painted in the 18th century by artists in Rajasthan, western India. They specialized in very fine, detailed work.

A MODERN TEMPLE

This modern temple is the Tulsi Manas Temple in Varanasi. It was built in 1964 in honor of the poet Tulsi Das (see page 29). You can see the tall *shikhara* tower rising up over the inner sanctum. Inside the temple, verses of Tulsi Das's great poem, the *Ram Charit Manas*, are carved in black on the white marble walls. This poem is based on the sacred *Ramayana*. Tulsi Das lived in Varanasi while he wrote his masterpiece.

✿ SYMBOLS ✿

Many different symbols appear in Hindu art. Each symbol has a special meaning.

The swastika symbol is an ancient sign of peace.

Om stands for perfection.

The lotus flower is a symbol of Vishnu.

The *Shri* symbol is a sign of wealth and well-being.

DO·HINDUS · LIKE · MUSIC·AND · DANCE?

Music and dancing are important parts of Hindu festivals and celebrations. Stories from the *Ramayana* and *Mahabharata* poems are often set to music or retold in dance to bring them alive. Dancers and musicians perform in temples and are asked to play at weddings. The audience often join in, clapping and singing along. Classical Hindu music and dance follow strict rules, which were first invented thousands of years ago. But there are many different styles of song and dance. These include the religious hymns, called *bhajans*, which are sung in temples, and the lively folk dances performed at festival times. Each region of India has its own special songs and dances.

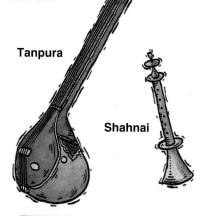

Tanpura

Shahnai

CLASSICAL MUSIC

From left to right, these musicians are playing the *tablas* (drums), the *sitar* (played like a guitar) and a *sarangi* (played with a bow, like a cello). They do not follow a set piece of music. Instead, Indian classical music is based on one of several melodies, called *ragas*. The musicians make up the rest of the music around the raga. Each raga has a different mood, such as sadness, bravery or love, and is suitable for a different time of day.

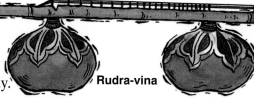

Rudra-vina

 MUSIC AND DANCE

The Indian sitar player, Ravi Shankar, has helped to make Indian classical music famous all over the world.

Some Hindi films contain as many as 18 songs and dances and can last for almost four hours.

An ancient book on classical dance lists 36 ways for dancers to raise and lower their eyes, eyelids and eyebrows in order to change their expression.

A raga is usually made up of between five and seven notes.

MUSICAL INSTRUMENTS

The classical musical instruments shown above are:

Shahnai – a wind instrument like an oboe, with seven holes.

Tanpura – a stringed instrument over three feet long, held upright in front of the musician.

Rudra-vina – a stringed instrument with two 'bowls'.

CHARACTER MAKE-UP

This Kathakali dancer is putting on his make-up before a performance. Each dancer has different-colored clothes and make-up, depending on whether he plays a hero, a villain, a king or a demon. Green means good, red means brave or fierce, black means evil and white pure.

HAND SIGNALS

In Indian classical dance, each gesture, or movement of the eyes, head and hands, has a special meaning. These hand positions are called *mudras*. The ones shown here are used in a style of classical dancing called Kathak. The audience can follow the story just by looking at the dancers' hand movements. It takes many years of training to become an Indian classical dancer. There are hundreds of *mudras* and other movements to learn.

Vishnu

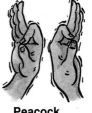

Shiva

Birds

KATHAKALI DANCERS

This is Kathakali dancing, a style of dance from South India. The dancers are all men. They wear elaborate costumes and masks to perform very dramatic dances based on the great Hindu poems. The larger-than-life characters leap across the stage to the sound of drums and cymbals. Some performances can last for 12 hours.

Peacock

Beautiful

Sorrowful

DO·HINDUS · L I K E · STORIES?

Yes, they do! The most popular stories come from the *Ramayana*, the *Mahabharata* and other sacred books. They tell of the exploits and adventures of gods such as Rama and Krishna. For thousands of years, before these tales were written down, storytellers learned the stories by heart and wandered from village to village reciting them. Storytellers are still popular at weddings and other celebrations. Hindu children hear these stories when they are very young. They can read them in comic books and watch them on television. This is one of the best-loved stories of all, about how Rama rescues Sita from the clutches of Ravana, demon king of Lanka.

THE STORY OF THE RAMAYANA

King Dasharatha was the king of Ayodhya, a city in northern India. Rama was the eldest of the king's four sons and heir to his throne. But Rama's stepmother had other plans. She wanted her son, Bharata, to be king and persuaded her husband to banish Rama from the kingdom for 14 years. Sadly, Rama did as he was told. He left his home and went to live in the forest with his wife, Sita, and his brother, Lakshman.

One day, while Rama and Lakshman were out hunting deer, Sita was kidnapped by the demon king of Lanka, the terrible, ten-headed Ravana. Rama and Lakshman searched the forest for several days. But Sita was nowhere to be found and Rama was broken-

RAVANA

Ravana was the evil, ten-headed demon king of Lanka, the island we call Sri Lanka. He had been told that if he married Sita he would become ruler of the world.

hearted. 'I will find her,' he vowed, 'if it's the last thing I do.' He asked his trusty friend, the monkey general, Hanuman, to help him. For Hanuman was leader of a great army and had many magical powers besides. Hanuman looked high and low, with no luck at all, until he reached the tip of India, right down in the south. There he met a vulture who told him that Ravana had taken Sita to his palace, many miles across the sea. But however could Hanuman cross the sea?

Now Hanuman was no ordinary monkey, but the son of the god of the wind. He took a huge, running leap and soared through the sky and over the sea to Lanka. He crept into Ravana's mighty palace and found Sita. She was being kept prisoner in the palace garden, surrounded by Ravana's demon guards. Hanuman told her that Rama would come to rescue her. Then he tried to get away, but the demon guards caught him and took him to Ravana, who tied him up with ropes of snakes and ordered the guards to set fire to his tail. Sita prayed to the gods to save him and this they did. With only a slightly singed tail to show for it, Hanuman leaped across the sea and back to Rama.

Rama and Lakshman gathered a huge army together, led by Hanuman and Jambhavan, king of the bears. They built a great bridge across the ocean to Lanka and marched across it to do battle. Ravana was waiting. He sent his best generals, giants and demons, to kill Rama, but Rama simply tossed them aside. Then Ravana sent an army of the most evil demons he could find. All night the battle raged and by morning the ground was stained with blood. Among the wounded lay Rama and Lakshman.

CAST LIST

King Dasharatha	Rama's father
Rama	an avatar of Vishnu, born on earth as a royal prince
Lakshman **Shatrughna** **Bharata** }	Rama's brothers
Sita	Rama's wife
Ravana	king of Lanka
Indrajit	Ravana's son
Jambhavan	king of the bears
Hanuman	the monkey god

Hanuman is a general in the monkey army who becomes Rama's faithful friend. He is also son of the wind god and has great strength, energy and wisdom.

Hanuman

Hanuman thought quickly. The only way to save them both was to get healing herbs from the top of a mountain. He leaped away, as fast as he could. When he returned, he gave the herbs to Rama and Lakshman and restored them both to health. The time had now come for Rama to face up to Ravana, alone. Ravana put on his silver armor, with a silver helmet on each of his heads, and raced in his war chariot right towards Rama. But Rama was ready. He fitted a golden arrow into his golden bow and fired it straight at Ravana's heart. With a terrible shriek and a howl of agony, Ravana toppled over and died.

Then Sita appeared from Ravana's palace and was reunited with Rama at last. Together with Lakshman and their faithful friend Hanuman, they returned home to Ayodhya, their exile over. There they were crowned king and queen, amid the greatest rejoicing there had ever been.

PLAY ACTING
The two children above are dressed up as Rama and Sita, ready to act out the story of the *Ramayana* during the festival of Dussehra (see page 33).

·GLOSSARY·

ARATI A tray of small lamps or incense burners offered to a god or goddess as a sign of welcome.

ARYANS A group of people who invaded India from the north-west in about 1500BC. Their religion, gods and sacred books were the starting point of Hinduism.

ASHRAM A place where Hindus can go to learn about their religion and to meditate. Ashrams are often attached to monasteries or temples.

ASHRAMA One of four stages in a Hindu's life. (Not to be confused with *ashram*.)

AVATAR A form taken by the god Vishnu on his visits to earth. The two most important avatars of Vishnu are Rama and Krishna.

AYURVEDA The ancient, traditional Hindu system of medicine.

BHAJAN A hymn or religious song.

BRAHMAN The supreme soul or spirit, which does not have any shape or form. (Not to be confused with the god Brahma, the creator of the world.)

DARSHANA The viewing or sight of the image of the god or goddess in the temple. The main purpose of a visit to a temple or shrine.

DEITY Another word for a god or goddess.

GHAT A step by a river from which people can bathe or where bodies are cremated.

GURU A religious teacher.

INNER SANCTUM The innermost shrine of a temple where the image of the god or goddess stands. The holiest part of the temple.

KARMA Your actions and their results.

LINGAM A stone or marble carving used to symbolize Shiva. (The plural is linga.)

MANDIR A Hindu temple.

MEDITATION Sitting quietly and focussing your mind on a word or picture to achieve inner calm or peace.

MOKSHA The freedom of the soul from the cycle of birth and rebirth. The aim of every Hindu's life.

PRASAD Food or flowers which are offered to the deity to be blessed. They are then returned to the worshipers to carry the deity's blessing back to them.

PUJA The form of worship carried out in a temple or shrine.

RAKHI A bracelet made of cotton or silk and decorated with baubles. Sisters tie rakhis around their brothers' wrists at the Raksha Bandhan festival in August.

REINCARNATION The belief that a person's soul is reborn in a different body when they die.

RITUAL A religious ceremony.

SADHU A Hindu holy man or saint.

SAMSARA The cycle of birth, death and rebirth.

SAMSKARA A special ceremony performed at an important time in a Hindu's life, such as birth, marriage or death.

SANATANA DHARMA How Hindus describe their set of beliefs, the 'eternal law' or 'eternal teaching'.

SANNYASIN A person who has given up their home and worldly belongings to live a life as a wandering monk.

SANSKRIT The ancient language of India and the sacred language of the holy books of Hinduism.

SWASTIKA The ancient Hindu sign of peace and good fortune. The word means 'it is well'.

TILAKA A mark made with red paste on a person's forehead as a sign of blessing.

TIRTHA A sacred place for Hindus, often near a river. A tirtha is believed to be a crossing place from this world to *moksha*.

YANTRA A special design or pattern which a person concentrates on to focus their mind as they meditate.

· I N D E X ·